Go 2 Work Now Summary

Are you ready to get the job you want?

Are you ready to make the necessary changes in life to make your dreams a reality?

Are you ready to live the life you have always wanted?

You Are On The Right Path

Go 2 Work Now will help you achieve your life goals.

This practical, no-nonsense book will help to push you beyond life's limitations and show you how to get what you think you can't have.

Struggling to find a job and overcoming your socio-economic conditions can be a daunting and difficult task. With this book you will have the necessary tools to not only get the job you desire, but to change your entire life in the process.

In the following pages you will learn how to:

- Tap into your inner-self and unleash your inner power
- Change your mind-set to overcome adversity
- Attract the right people in your life
- Positively influence those around you to create synergy
- Learn which careers are felony proof

In addition you will get a better understanding of yourself by accessing your strengths & weaknesses, block out negativity, and create a focused concentration of energy that will provide you with stimulation, opportunity, and success. Most of all this book will help you

Be The Best You Can Be

Proceeds from the sale of this will go to support Sunshine Ministries Inc a non-profit domestic abuse/ Prison Ministry

Go 2 Work
NOW

The Ex-offenders' Guide to Getting the
Job You Want *Now* and More!

Eric R. Stuckey

To order additional copies of this book, contact:
Xlibris Corporation
1-888-795-4274
www.Xlibris.com
Orders@Xlibris.com
100796

Contents

Acknowledgments 7

Introduction..9

PART ONE

Out of Chaos Comes Order 17

Renewing of Your Mind 24

Six a Day: The Formula for Success.....................................28

This Is Life Changing...29

The Value of an Education 31

Get It! The Government Is Paying You to Work 34

How to Get a Job with a Felony Record 36

Building Your Own Brand..38

The Market Analysis 40

Getting Ready for the Job You Want 41

Set a Goal to Help You Reach the Top.................................43

Getting the Job You Want When You Want It! 45

Schedule Your Job Search 47

The Interview...52

Creating Your Future...54

Start Your Own Business 55

Planning for Your Future..56

How I Did It...60

Certified Green 64

Government Grants 65

Contents

Acknowledgments

No one has ever accomplished anything without
the help of others.
—Velma M. Stuckey

When it came time to express my appreciation to those who contributed to the realization of this project, my mind was in complete turmoil. Not because I didn't have anyone to thank but because so many contributed to this work in their own, unique way that I had no idea where to begin. Finally, it dawned on me that everyone I had the privilege of calling a friend has contributed in some way to the creation of this book. Here I will make an attempt to thank each of you for your contributions and support in my life.

First and foremost, I thank God, for without him, nothing would be possible in my life. It is by his spirit that the inspiration and resources to complete this work came about.

To my late mother, Velma M. Stuckey, who was and still is my rock. It was your love and nurturing that gave me the desire and strength to conquer life's challenges. I will love and miss you for the rest of my life!

Many thanks to my children: Aaron M. Woodson, Eric R. Stuckey lll, Octavian J. Stuckey, Aubrianna Thomas, Dominique Stuckey, and Malik Stuckey. I love you all, and if I can do this, imagine what you can do!

Thanks to my brothers: Dyrell Stevens, Albert l. Monroe, Carl l. Monroe, and Vernon J. Stuckey—for believing in me.

To Patricia Thomas, for bending over backward for me; lady, you are the best!

To my cousins Frank and Eva Polite, nephew Jamaco Taylor, Lewanna Stuckey Jordan, Elizabeth Stuckey, Jacinda Briggs, Tisha Nicole Henley, Bridgette Boddie, Wanda Shinholster, Jerome a.k.a. Harry, Ronald

Lawrence, and the Enclave on Cushman. My stepchildren, Joshwa and Jessica Hackney, thank you all for your love and support. Special thanks again to my brother, Vernon J. Stuckey. See, bro? I love you so much, I had to thank you twice (ha, ha).

Special thanks to the Georgia Department of Corrections! Your efforts in helping to rehabilitate ex-offenders have been critical in developing this book. Also, additional thanks to the Georgia Department of Labor, Floyd County, and Troup County probation department. Your staff truly inspired me to develop this work. May God bless you all!

Introduction

I vividly remember the gavel tapping the bench prior to being led from the courtroom. My case was quickly tried and disposed of in record time. The process was so fast that my mind didn't have a chance to fully comprehend what had taken place. I was told good luck then escorted from the courtroom. *What in the world had just happened?* Did the judge just sentence me to two years in prison? Just the thought of serving time made my heart beat a million miles a minute with no intention of slowing down. My vision became blurred. My head began to spin. How in the hell could this have happened to me I thought to myself. How could God not answer all those prayers I prayed? From the way things turned out he must not have heard them.

I glanced back at my lawyer to get some kind of reassurance that everything was going to be alright however he had already moved on to his next victim. As the deputy and I approached the side door that connected the court room to the jail, in walked another deputy with handcuffs in one hand and shackles in the other. From the look on his face I knew the jailhouse jewelry was for me. Our stride halted I was told to face the wall and put my hands behind my back. With jewelry now on I realized that my nightmare was real. I was no longer a free man, I was now a unwilling ward of the state.

Subsequently I was led to central processing (Intake) where I would be finger-printed, then booked into the jail system. Afterwards would come a shower then issuance of uniform. At the cell door the deputy raised his hand and like magic the door slid open. I was placed inside the cell where my wrist and leg jewelry were removed. Inside were two gentleman that smelled as if the bathed at the local dump. One was standing in the corner the other sitting with his face clasped in his hand. The place was cold almost to the point of freezing. As the deputy exited the room the doors slid shut. I watched sorrowfully as he walked away. It was in that widow, in that moment that I knew there would be no turning back I was here for the long haul. With fear in my heart and sorrow in my soul I took my place on the cold piece of steel that served as a bench. As I watched the hours pass many warm bodies were added to the small depository. Before I realized it, the place had filled to capacity.

What was once a cold abyss had now become a place of anguish, a fiery hell that none of us could escape. Tensions were high; Fear masked our faces as if we all was celebrating Halloween. None of us wanted to be there, but all had to embrace the fact that we were there in addition to we would be staying for awhile.

Each sat, trying not to stare at the others. The room was silent. No one uttered a word. We all just sat there trying to make some sense of it all. The silence caused me to drift away. Next thing I knew I was adrift in the world of Sleep It was in that state that I heard a voice calling for me in the distance. My eyes sprung open! I jumped to my feet scanning my surroundings in an attempt to put a face to the voice. To my disappointment, the room was just as quiet as it was before I left. *It was just a hallucination!* I said to myself. Sorrowfully, I readjusted my body to the cold slender steel. Within minutes, I was once again drifting toward the place I had left moments ago. Suddenly, I heard the voice again. This time it was no hallucination; this time it was real. Before I could get to my feet, the cell door slid open. The same deputy that brought me to this place had now re-appeared. *You're attorney would like to speak with you he exclaimed.* My despair had now turned to hope. *They had made a mistake, and now I would be vindicated,* I thought to myself.

As if by magic, my mojo had returned. There was pep in my step as I strolled down the corridor behind the officer. He led me to a room where my lawyer was present. Instantly a smile came across my face when I saw him. *This guy had come through for me after all,* I thought to myself as he turned to approach me. "Have a seat!" he said as he pulled the file from his briefcase. "Man, am I glad to see you again," I said before sitting down. In that moment, I was so sure everything had worked out to my advantage that any and all thoughts of what had taken place inside the courtroom had vanished. I was now going to be a free man. Thoughts of prison had been replaced by thoughts of how much celebrating I was going to do when I got home.

"What time am I being released?" were the first words to exit my mouth. He stood there with a confident smile, then started his conversation with

"Eric, let me explain to you what's going to happen next." Suddenly, my heart went into overdrive and my future back to the land of uncertainty.

"Eric, I am afraid the judge's decision is final" was all I heard before being transported to another world. A world where I was free, a world where I could do no wrong, and if I did, I would only receive slaps on the wrist. I had a chance to enjoy that alternate universe where everything was perfect for only a brief moment.

Soon after arriving, I was snatched back by another familiar voice. But this time, it wasn't my lawyer; it was the deputy informing us that our time was up. As I stood to exit, my mind still in a daze, my lawyer said to me, "Don't worry about anything. You will be out in eight months, and everything will be back to normal!" That was easy for him to say. He wasn't the one who had to sit in hell for those eight months.

To save time; lets just say that everything he told me was a complete lie I ended up doing twenty-one of the twenty-four-month sentence. Since it was my first felony I was sentenced to a detention center instead of a state prison. There I spent my time reflecting on the error of my ways and telling everyone I could about the word of God. Admitingly my stay wasn't all bad. In-fact everything was as good as it could have been considering I was incarcerated. By focusing on Gods word I began to see life a lot different than I use too. I was riding the wave of positive change. I guess you could say I had become a holy roller. That is until I got the phone call that completely changed my life forever.

I was called to the counselors office for what I thought was a routine vist to discuss my future plans after prison. However when I arrived he wasn't his usual happy self. This time he had a somber look on his face. I was told I had an emergency phone call. Again heart beating a million miles a minute I picked up the phone. All I heard was "Momma is dead" after that I blacked out. I came to about three days later, my life no longer the same. At first I thought I had dreamed the whole thing but the straight jacket I was in told a different story. Turns out it was true, the apple of my eye was no-longer with me. My brother said she was killed during a home invasion. They knocked her uncounscious before robbing her and then setting the house on fire to cover it up. Who would do such a thing? Who would kill someone who gave so much of themselves to help others? The bright-side was that my son who was living with her at the time wasn't there, if so it would have been two bodies instead of one. I was thankful to God for sparing his life!

As the months went by the police did there best to find her killer. (Douglas County deputy's and investigaters are A-1) Again I was called to the counselors office! Again it was my brother, and again I woke-up in a straight jacket. Because this is a hurtful subject for me to talk about I will keep it short and simple. The person responsible for her death turned out to be my son. My very own flesh and bloodWhen I first found out that he was responsible for her death, my body went numb. Surely they had made a mistake! It couldn't be, not my son! My life was in chaos. I couldn't eat or sleep.

Turned out it was true. He was the killer and all because she wouldn't allow him to attend a friend's party. To make matters worse he never admitted his guilt, even when shown his picture buying the gas that was used to burn down the house. During the trial, he chose not to take the stand. Instead, he sat there during the proceedings, drawing circles on pieces of paper. Ultimately He was found guilty, then sentenced to life plus twenty years in prison. To make matters worse, he was only fifteen when he committed the crime.

As you can see, the statement my lawyer had made years earlier about everything being back to normal when I get out turned out to be a bunch of bullshit, to say the least. When I exited prison, I was given a $25 debit card, a pat on the back by the warden, and another "wish you luck" from my counselor before being escorted to the chain-link gate that led to freedom. Now that this chapter in my life was over, it was time to face the chaos that dwelt in the next: a life without a mother, my child imprisoned, and a family that now despised me because of my son's involvement in her death.

As I passed through those prison gates, which separated my past from my future, I again heard a voice calling for me in the distance. This time, it was one that brought joy to my heart. As I looked across the wide parking lot, I found its point of origin. It was the voice of my brother and his pastor. So much time had passed since I last saw him; he looked different from what I had remembered. With arms stretched wide, we ran toward each other as if we were long-lost loved ones, then embraced in brotherly love. All things said, he appeared to be happy to see me despite the circumstances that now surrounded our lives; however, his facial expressions told of a different story. They told of the agony and despair that loomed in his heart as well as his mind. I couldn't help but feel the pain that emanated from the depths of his soul because the same pain was inside me.

As we drove back to Atlanta, the ride was quiet, no one uttering a word. As the miles past, I couldn't help but think on what life would be like without my mother. During that time, I couldn't help but think how life would be without her here to encourage me. The thought sent tears rolling down my face! By the time we entered the city, I had come to the conclusion that I would make my mother proud by living a life of empowerment—a life that would not only bring about positive change in my own life but one that would also help change the lives of others. I was determined to do things bigger and better than before; I would take life by the horns and make it submit to my will. To start, I would get a job, then use that as a stepping stone in building her ministry. All her life she dedicated her time and money to Sunshine Ministries, which was and still is dedicated to changing the lives of offenders and ex-offenders across the country.

I had the skills, all I needed was the right vehicle to accomplish my mission. Prior to being incarcerated I was a successful mortgage broker and real estate investor. I had also helped in the creation of sunshine ministries along with my mothers many business instrest., With those skills, I couldn't lose even if the economy was in the tank. I was sure I could find a way to help people like myself overcome lifes adversities all I needed was a foundation, but right now I needed to report to my parole officer. I was told I had five days to do so, but would do it today. Not only that, but I was determined to have a job by the end of the week. I was on the fast track to success, and nothing was going to keep me from getting where I wanted to go. I walked into the parole office with my head in the clouds. My parole officer greeted me, then gave me some great advice on staying out of trouble and the importance of paying my mothly feesI walked out of those doors just as confident as I was before I went in. Everything was going to be all right; my plan was already in motion. Next step was to find a job. I started the week with a bang. I answered every ad in the newspaper, filled out countless applications, but all to no avail. No one would give me the time of day; however, there were a few companies that did call me in for an interview. But when the question of Have you ever had a felony conviction? came up during the conversation, my interviews came to a halt with the ever-so-familiar phrase "I will give you a call, thanks for coming by" at the end.

This process continued for months with no job in sight! At the end of three months, I had to ask myself, what was I doing wrong? I had followed the counselor's advice on how to get a job, but none of those tactics worked.

I decided to speak with my PO concerning my situation; maybe he could point me in the right direction. I sat in the parole department's lobby for two hours, awaiting that push in the right direction. Finally, the push did come, but not from the source I was seeking it from.

As I sat there waiting, I listened as parolee after parolee conversed with one another concerning how hard it was for them to find employment. It was then that a light went off in my head. I would do research on what employers wanted in an employee; then, I would use the information to find myself a job and then help others do the same by duplicating my steps.

During my research, I not only found a way to gain employment but also discovered solid techniques that I could learn that would guarantee me success in every area of my life. Those techniques that helped me to overcome the greatest adversity in my life and that helped me get where I am today are the same techniques I am giving you. My hope is that this book will help you get the job you need and to help build a solid foundation for your new life. Be blessed, and remember, "Fortune favors the bold!"

Part One

Out of Chaos Comes Order

Chaos is defined as "complete confusion and disorder," a state in which behavior and events are not controlled by anything.

Right now you are probably thinking that your life is in a state of chaos, that everything around you is spinning out of control. You made a mistake in your past, paid for that mistake, and now you are putting forth your best effort toward turning your life around. But it seems that no matter how hard you try, you always end up back at square one.

Let me say that you are not alone. Just about everyone in the world has and will experience what you are feeling right now. Everyone will experience the unexpected, that sudden occurrence that will throw your life completely out of order. It could be the untimely passing of a loved one, suffering an accident, or making poor choices in life that led to jail, prison, or probation/parole. All these things and many more can result in our lives being thrown out of sync.

Though this may be your present situation, it is not the end of the world. What you have to do now is learn from your past mistakes and use what you have experienced to find solutions that will help you to live a more dynamic life.

It is a known fact that out of chaos, order comes. Don't believe me? Here are a few examples of individuals who has experienced chaos (great adversity), overcame, and then went on to accomplish great things in their lives.

Bernard Hopkins Jr. a.k.a. the Executioner is considered by many to be the best middleweight champion ever. He was the first fighter to retain all four world titles of each major sanctioning body plus _The Ring_ belt in the same fight, but did you know that Mr. Hopkins was an ex-felon just like you? That's right! Bernard Hopkins Jr., considered the best middleweight ever by many, went to prison when he was seventeen years old. He was sentenced to eighteen years but was released on parole after serving five years. While in prison, he took an interest in boxing as a way to pass the time. Once out, he realized that boxing could be the way out of his chaotic surroundings and lifestyle.

Once released, he decided to focus his attention on boxing, desiring to become the best boxer he could be despite his late start in the profession. Day after day, he focused his attention on his intentions, choosing to train rather than hang with his old friends, work instead of crime. Then on April 29, 1995, Bernard Hopkins Jr. (ex-felon) became a world champion by knocking out Segundo Mercado of Ecuador in the seventh round. Hopkins had now realized his goal. All that training had paid off. He was champion of the world! But Bernard didn't stop there. Now that he had achieved his goal, he set another goal, one that was greater than the first. He decided that he would be the undisputed middleweight champion of the world by unifying all belts in his weight class. Guess what? He did that too!

Can you imagine how hard it must have been for Mr. Hopkins to not get caught up into the negativity that's often associated with prison? How hard it must have been for him to leave old friends and maybe some family members alone? What it took for him to reach deep within and tap into his higher self? To say, "I will not going to let anything or anyone hold me down." So what if I went to prison? So what if I have a felony record? Bernard said, "I ain't never going back to prison again!" I am going to make life better for me and for my children. Just like Bernard, you too must make the same decision to focus on your intentions, making sure to stay focused on overcoming adversity to accomplish your goals.

His life was in chaos! But he decided to embrace his current circumstances and use them to transform his life in a positive way. Instead of allowing his past to hinder his life, he chose to use it to create new possibilities for himself. He turned a life of bitter lemons into refreshing lemonade, and you can do the same. Like Bernard and countless other ex-offenders, you have the same opportunity to take the chaos that life has thrown you and use it to your advantage.

If you will accept the fact that you made a mistake and that that mistake has caused your present situation (chaotic) and that you are going to make the most out of where you are, what you have, and use it to your advantage, then you are well on your way to turning your chaotic situation/life into order (positive change). Would you believe me if I told you that your world is a direct reflection of you, of who you are on the inside? Whether you believe me or not, it's true. Everything that's taking place right now in your life is because of whom you have chosen to be on the inside.

I read a book entitled *Harmonic Wealth* by James Arthur Ray. In it he explains that our results are the direct outcomes of our thoughts, feelings, and consistent behaviors. In order for us to take control of our lives, first we have to take control over our behavior. Only by doing this can we take control of our destiny. If you really want to turn your chaotic life into something more, then you have to be willing to do the things that are necessary to make it happen.

> Every man got the right to his own mistakes. Ain't no
> man that ain't made any?
>
> —Joe Louis

Let me start by emphasizing that this book was not written for inspirational purposes only. Its main purpose is to help you get a job fast; however, it's more than that! It's also a guide to help you become a better you. If you're looking for inspiration only, then you need to stop right now and go purchase something by Dr. Creflo Dollar or Bishop T. D. Jakes. What I'm giving you here is more than an uplifting word. What I am giving you here is the recipe to a better future.

Over the last three years, the United States has been in one of the worst recessions since the stock market crash of 1929, which left millions of Americans out of work. And now over eighty years later, we are back in the same situation, and for some, it's even worse.

With so many Americans unemployed and Congress slashing the budgets of many domestic programs, it's now more difficult than ever for ex-offenders to receive the help they so desperately need.

In a July 2, 2010, report by CNNMoney.com, it says that the US unemployment rate is steadily hovering around 9 percent and that it would take the creation of 10.6 million jobs immediately for the population to be working as was the case three years ago. In fact, the Federal Reserve estimates that unemployment will stay around 7 percent or above through 2012 and in the 5 to 5.3 percent range after.

When hearing statistics like this each day, whether online, in your local newspaper, or on local and national news stations, it's hard not to become disillusioned. In addition to this, you must consider that the vast majority of these unemployed individuals don't have criminal records and are still having a difficult time finding employment. So with that said, let me ask you a question. How hard do you think it is for someone like you to get a job? Normally, after posing a question like this, the answer would be "slim to nonexistent." However, since you have bought my book, the answer is now "not hard at all." Why? Because now you have made the first step in going from where you are to where you want to be by purchasing my book.

See, society as a whole has more to worry about than you. Times are so hard now that even those few individuals or companies that have advocated for ex-offender rights in the past are now more preoccupied with keeping themselves above water than with the plight of someone who has unfortunately made some bad choices in their life. With that said, you can now understand that in order for you to make it, especially after you have been incarcerated or convicted of any crime other than minor traffic violations, you will need *help*, and I am here to give it to you. However, before I get too far along, let me tell you how what you are about to read came to be.

Earlier I told you how I started out just like you. The only difference between us is, like Bernard Hopkins Jr., I decided to make a change in my life. I was determined to put a plan into motion that would help propel my life to a new level, and you have the same potential as I do. You just need a place to start, and I am giving it to you.

Since my release, I have had the privilege of helping many ex-offenders improve their quality of life. Whether it was advice on landing a good job, starting a new business, or tips on the best careers to study for in school, I have always done my best to help those individuals succeed.

Right now you're probably thinking, what makes you so special? The answer is *nothing*! I'm just a guy who has been where you are, experienced what you have experienced, and found a way to beat the odds; and all I want to do is help you become better without the trials and errors that come along with such a task.

It's because I have been in the same situation that you're in right now that I am able to help you. That's right; the reason I'm able to help people like you is that I have walked in your shoes and experienced your pain. I know what it's like to go out every day hoping someone will give you a chance to make a living.

Long ago, I made a few mistakes in life that resulted in a felony conviction. It was after I had spent two years in prison that I found out how hard it really is for ex-offenders to find a job.

When I was released, my mind was set on conquering the world. I hit the pavement armed with all the advice and training I had received in prison on how to reintegrate into society and find a job.

I was told during my four-hour reentry class that when applying for a job, always put in "Will discuss at interview!" on the "Have you ever been convicted of a felony?" section. If you have done it, then you already know this is a bunch of crap. No employer wants to discuss a thing with you at the interview because nine times out of ten, you are not going to make it to the interview stage unless you know the person giving the interview (the employer) or have friends or family within the organization and in that case the interview would be only a formality. If not, then they're going to toss your application aside as soon as you leave. There were occasions during my job search when I wasn't given an application due to being asked about any felony convictions beforehand.

It was only after experiencing so many humiliating situations like these that I thought to myself, *There must be a way around this problem. And if I am having this kind of trouble getting a job, imagine what others like me are going through.* That's when I decided to do some research concerning my situation. I didn't have a computer, so I went to the nearest public library. I found a lot of books about how to find a job, but none that truly applied to people in our situation. I decided to try the Internet to see what I could find there. I typed in "jobs for ex-offenders." The search engine churned out a long list of books and charitable organizations for me to choose from.

Out of desperation, I clicked on a few sites to see what they were offering and decided to make a few calls, but to no avail. Either they weren't offering any help in my area, they were out of money, or were gone out of business. Though disappointed, I refused to give up.

I continued my search; however, my goals changed. Now instead of focusing my attentions on myself, I broadened my horizons to include everyone who was experiencing what I was experiencing. Because of my desire to help not only myself but also help others, I now was more determined than ever to help people like me get the second chance in life we so desperately needed.

Through tireless research, I found that although there were a large number of companies that didn't hire ex-felons, there were many who would give someone like you and me a chance if I could show myself to be the right person for the position. I had to separate the person I was now from the individual I was before.

As I gathered information for this book, I learned that if you had a felony or some misdemeanors, a certain amount of years would have had to have passed since the felony conviction before an employer would even think about giving you a chance. Usually it was seven to ten years. This requirement alone makes finding a job extremely difficult for ex-offenders.

I also found that one major reason employers give for not hiring ex-felons is due to insurance reasons. Most HR managers I have spoken with say it's just too hard to get insurance companies to insure someone with a felony record. However, the main reason for felons not gaining employment is a *lack of understanding*. Many HR managers simply don't know how to deal with an ex-offender. One of the first thoughts that come to their mind is that the person sitting in front of them is violent, steals, and will cause trouble on the job.

On the contrary, violent offenders only make up a small percentage of the ex-felons in the country, and the vast majority of ex-offenders are nonviolent.

Statistics have shown that an ex-offender's ability to find employment is consistent with high recidivism rates. Over the years, the federal and state governments have enacted legislation to help an ex-offender reintegrate into society; however, many of the programs that have been established do little, if anything at all, to bring about real change in the ex-offender's life, which in turn brings about a lack of self-esteem, causing many to return to a life of crime just to make a living.

I wrote this book so you, me, and countless others can finally be free from the torment of going in circles when looking for a job and get our lives back on track. I want each and every one of my fellow brothers and sisters out there who has made some mistakes to have a chance to live a life without limits. I want you to be successful, and if I can help you to help yourself, then I have succeeded in what I set out to accomplish.

However, as with anything else in life, the information that you receive here is only as good as the amount of effort you're willing to put behind it. In other words, if you don't use it, it won't produce the results it was designed to produce. But if you follow the instructions in this book, I guarantee it will help you to restructure your life and to develop good work habits that will not only help you to get the job you want, but will also show you how to succeed in life beyond your wildest dreams.

The steps that I am about to reveal to you here are the same ones that I used to get to where I am today. The only difference is that you don't have to make the same mistakes that I did. In fact, with the knowledge you will receive in the following pages, you will have everything you need to get a job, retain it, and become successful in other areas of your life.

You may be asking yourself, How is following what I have done going to get you the same results? Good question! To answer you, let's take a look at McDonald's. They have thousands of stores across the world. However, each store operates in the same way as all the rest do. The burgers are the same, fries are the same, everything the same. The only difference that may occur is that in some places, the name of a particular item may be changed in order for that item to represent that country's language. The process that McDonald's and so many other businesses use to succeed is called duplication, which means "the act or process of copying something."

This means that every McDonald's operates as those before it, and by doing so, they obtain the same results—*success*. Well, just as each McDonald's uses the same recipe to the letter to produce the same results, so it is for you. If you want successful results, then you have to follow someone who has been where you are, has done what you are trying to do, and has arrived to the place you want to get to.

You may also say in your mind, *Well, how do I know you are successful?* My answer to that question is, "You're reading the book I have written." Is that answer good enough for you?

Now with that behind us, let's get started!

As you read through this book and apply the techniques, you will begin to see positive changes in every area of your life. I am giving you all the tools you will need to (1) renew your mind to bring forth positive energy in your daily life; (2) get the job you want, no matter your background; (3) learn how to excel on your job; (4) restore your credit rating; (5) take advantage of government money to help you succeed; and (6) use other people's money to start your own business. When you are finished, you will be armed with the all the weapons you will need to conquer your three worst enemies: *yourself, fear,* and *lack of resources.* There is nothing in this book that you can't do from the comfort of your own home. The only other thing you will need besides this book is a real desire to succeed.

Now sit back, relax, and allow the information you are about to read change your life forever.

Renewing of Your Mind

In every adversity, look for the benefit that can come out of it. Even bad experiences offer benefits, but you have to look for them.

—Eric V. Copage

The statement made above is so true. In this life, we will go through adversity, some more than others. However, no matter the amount of adversity you go through, remember in the end that we are responsible for the lives we live and we are ultimately responsible for its outcome.

No matter what situation you are in right now, you still have a choice to either stay where you are or go on to something else; it's all up to you. If you choose to read the information in this book and do nothing with it, then that is your prerogative, and hopefully things will still work out for you in the long run. However, if you choose to take this information and apply it, I assure you that you will accomplish anything and everything you set out to do.

The first step in achieving what you want is to get your mind conditioned to take on the task at hand. In other words, you have to begin the process of renewing your way of thinking.

Many of you who have grown up in the church have probably already heard the phrase "renewing your mind," but do you really know what it means?

It means that you must restore, regenerate, and change the way you think, which in turn will change the way you act. If you think in a negative manner, then sooner or later, your actions will begin to reflect your negative way of thinking. This, in turn, will begin to bring about negative circumstances and results in your life. However, on the other end of the spectrum, if you begin the process of training your mind to think in a positive manner, then the circumstances in your life will begin to emulate your new mind-set.

For example, if you sit around all day thinking thoughts like "I will never find a job because of my record" or "I know people who have college degrees and they can't find a job. how is it impossible for me to find one."

These are some of the most common phrases I have heard from people from all walks of life, and they wonder why things aren't working out for them.

When you allow your mind to think in this way, you have already begun to cancel out any possibility of anything positive coming your way, especially a job.

Now I am not saying that all you have to do is think positively and everything is going to fall into place; there is a little more to it than that. It's also going to take some initiative on your part. You will have to start retraining the way you think by first changing things you do and changing the people you hang around with.

I am not telling you to get rid of everyone in your life, but I am saying you must distance yourself from individuals who mean you no good.

Someone once said, "Everyone that is good with you ain't necessarily good for you."

There may be people in your past or in your present life that you get along with, have fun with, and enjoy being around with. Some you may have grown up with, but sometimes, these same individuals, though they may be cool to hang around with, they will end up holding you back in the long run. They may mean well, but the truth is, you are trying to make a positive change; and if they are bringing negativity into your life, it's best to rid yourself of them now than to allow their presence to hinder your new walk. In order for you to make it, you're going to essentially have to become a new person altogether.

In the Bible, God told Abram, "Get out of your country, from your kindred and from your father's house, to a land that I will show you. I will make you a great nation; I will bless you and make your name great; and you shall be a blessing. I will bless those who bless you, and I will curse him who curses you; and in you all the families of the earth shall be blessed" (Gen. 12:1-3).

Abram's father, Terah, had moved the family from the city of Ur, to the city of Haran. Now in Haran, I am sure that Abram made new friends. Some of them probably seemed to be good friends to Abram, but God saw something that Abram couldn't see. God saw that the friends Abram had were not good for him in the long run. They were holding him back and would have held him back from becoming the man God had created him to be. And the Bible goes on to say that once God told Abram what he needed to do, Abram left those old friends and life behind and went on to become a very wealthy man. He also became the father of all who have *faith*. What is *faith*? Faith believes that the outcome already is, even though everything around you says that it isn't.

Abram had believed what God had said and was blessed beyond measure, and just like Abram was blessed, so can you be. But first, you have to separate yourself from the people in your life who mean you no good because if you don't, they will end up holding you back and keeping you in bondage! God does not want this for you, and neither do I.

You may be saying right now, "What does this have to do with me getting a job?" Well, the answer is simple: before you can move on to a bright, new future, you first have to leave the old self, friends, and way of thinking behind. In other words, no matter how you have thought, lived, or performed in the past, it is just that, all in the past; and in order for you to fully achieve your true potential in this world, you have to make right changes and move forward.

I read a book once entitled *A New Earth* by Eckhart Tolle. In it, he talks about how your mind works in relation to your life.

He states that "you don't become good by trying to be good, but by finding the goodness that is already within you and allowing that goodness to emerge." But the good in your life that you are trying to obtain can only come about if something changes in the way you think. Even the Bible confirms that an individual can and will be changed by the renewing of their mind-set.

"And do not be conformed to this world, but be transformed [changed] by the renewing of your mind, that you may prove [show yourself and those around you] what is that good and acceptable and perfect will of God."

Understand that God did not create you to live a life of lack. He created you to live a life without limits. And *it doesn't matter what you have done in the past*; you can have a better future. Right now you might be saying, "But you don't know some of the things I have done in life," and you know what? I don't. But guess what? It doesn't matter! You still have the ability to stop the endless cycle that you are on by choosing to "think and live in a positive manner." Whatever that thing is, leave it there in the past, and make a commitment right now to change and to walk in that change no matter what.

I understand how negative your thought process can be once you have been incarcerated. As I told you before, I have been there myself! You begin to develop this mind-set that it's you against the world and that there is no one looking out for you, so why bother to do anything except what you have been doing? Hey, it put money in my pocket, food on the table, and clothes on my back; so it wasn't all bad! Yes, that may be true, but it also got you put in jail, made it *almost* impossible for you to now get a job and provide for yourself and your children.

When I was released, I experienced those same types of thoughts and displayed the same type of attitude, but I decided that I was going to do something about it. I was not going to let life hold me back. I was not going to be separated from my kids and family ever again. I had to make a decision to *change*. Did I have everything at my disposal to make that change? Of course not! I didn't have a computer or transportation, so I borrowed some money for a bus pass, then went to the public library and found every book I could on changing the way you think.

I learned from those books that I didn't have to live the way I was living. I was worth more than what was on my record. I came to understand that I was a victim of self, and the only way to change self was to begin telling myself that "I am more than a conquer!"

I began a process called reaffirmation, which simply means "to make new again"; and that's exactly what I intended to do, make myself new again. I learned that if I would simply start training my mind to think differently on a daily basis, everything in my life would begin to change. I started telling myself over and over again, "Eric, you're a winner, not a loser!" I began to act like a winner by removing those individuals in my life who meant me no good, and as time passed, my life began to produce results like a winner. And guess what? Now I *am* a winner, and if I can do it, so can you. But first, you have to come to terms with yourself. You have to recognize that you have a certain level of dysfunction in your life and thought process and that it is this dysfunctional way of thinking that has ultimately brought about the events in your past, and for many of you, this pattern of thinking is still affecting your life. Will what I am talking about bring about positive change overnight? *No!* But if you keep at it, it will bring about the change that you need to reach your peak potential.

Six a Day: The Formula for Success

I read this story once that helped me change my life forever, and it might well change yours.

At the turn of the last century, a man named Ivy Lee met with Charles M. Schwab, president of Bethlehem Steel. His aim was to sell his services to Mr. Schwab and help him become more efficient. Schwab's response to Lee's offer was that his people already knew what to do; his problem was getting them to do it. Lee wasn't deterred by Schwab's remark. Instead, he responded to Schwab's statement with a statement of his own: "Suppose I could give you a tool, an action that would guarantee your company's efficiency. Would you be interested?" Schwab, though resistant, allowed Lee to continue. "What if I just give you the idea—let you use it for twenty-one days? If it works, share it with your employees, then send me a check for whatever you think it's worth." Schwab jumped at the opportunity, especially since he had nothing to lose and everything to gain.

This Is Life Changing

"At the end of the day before the following day, take out a piece of paper and write down the six most important things you need to do to achieve your objectives on that particular day," Lee said. "In fact, go ahead and do that right now for tomorrow." Schwab did it!

Now put them in order of importance: one being the most important, two being the second most important, and three being the next. Continue until you have six items on your list.

First thing tomorrow, start on item number one. Do not go to item number two until you have fully completed item number one. Then continue in succession with each number. If you get to the end of the day and have not completed your full list of items, then roll over your uncompleted items into the next day. Example: if items five and six are left one day, they automatically become items one and two for the next. Use this as long as you like, and then if you think it's worth something, send me a check for that amount.

Less than a month later, Lee received a check in the mail for $25,000 along with a note signed by Mr. Schwab. It read, "That's the most powerful tool for achievement that anyone has ever taught me, and here's a fraction of what it's worth."

Charles M. Schwab went on to amass a $100,000,000 fortune, making him one of the richest men alive. If that process was good enough for Charles M. Schwab, then it's good enough for me and should be good enough for you too.

Now I want you to start your six daily action steps. Remember to start with the most important thing you have to accomplish that day, then the next most important. Continue in this sequence until you have completed your list. If you don't complete all six action steps, roll the ones that weren't completed over to the following day. Be sure to complete the actions from the previous day first before starting your other task.

Word of caution: There are going to be distractions that will try to keep you from completing your action steps. Don't allow anything or anyone to get in your way. You have to stay focused on the prize. That's getting a job, getting an education, and becoming a success.

The Value of an Education

Unfortunately in society today, I see so many talented individuals that have made past mistakes pay for those mistakes over and over again long after repaying their debt to society. Many times, society as a whole doesn't seem to want to forgive and forget. Instead, they prefer to condemn these individuals on a continuous basis.

Much has been written in the past decade concerning the plight of those who have been incarcerated; however, most of those books have been directed more toward inspiration instead of tackling the real issue that affects so many of us—that is, making a living once we integrate back into society.

When an individual is broke long enough, no matter how good their intentions, it can often lead to brokenness of spirit. This in turn leads to destructive thought patterns and actions that, if not curbed, will lead to that person ending up in a much-worse situation than before. It's time to "stop the madness."

The only true way for people like us to regain a foothold in life is through education. I can't stress enough how important it is for those of us who have been incarcerated to obtain a proper education. An education drastically reduces the chances of an ex-offender committing another offense and improves their chances of becoming productive members of society again.

It's a known fact that the better the education, the better your chances of survival.

Fact: Did you know that people with criminal backgrounds are one of the fastest-growing minorities in the nation?

As a convicted felon, you must gain as much knowledge and training as possible in order to achieve your goals. Gone are the days when you could get by using brawn alone. Now you have to use both brawn and brains to maximize your results. Learning a new skill or brushing up on existing skills is now more important than ever.

Because you have a record, which counts as two strikes against you in itself. In addition, being certified in a particular field will help you to stand out from the rest. It says to your perspective employer that you really have put your old ways behind you and are attempting to live a positive life.

Society as a whole tends to stand behind those who make an effort to overcome adversity. Some of the most successful movies in Hollywood have been about the underdog overcoming all odds to win in the end. Remember the movie *Bait*, starring Jamie Foxx. In it, he plays a criminal that goes to jail for robbery; and through a series of fortunate events, along with a real desire to change, he ends up overcoming all obstacles and setbacks to win in the end.

Just like his character, who in the midst of chaos learned something of value and that particular something turned out to be just what he needed to help him win in the end, so it is with you.

You have to learn that particular something in your life, that skill that will help propel you to new heights; however, you can't just study anything and think life will be a walk in the park from here on out.

Depending on what's on your record, there are certain fields of study that should be avoided. Certain charges in your background can prevent you from working in certain fields. Depending on the type of convictions you have on your record, there are certain trades that would be of no benefit. For instance, if you have been convicted of a sex crime, studying to be a teacher would be a complete waste of time since you would have to register, and you won't be able to work around kids of any age. Drug offenses will probably bar you from anything in the medical field. Also, if you have a felony conviction period, there is no hope of you having a career in law enforcement unless the crime was committed as a juvenile. And even then, your record would have to been sealed.

Face it, as a convicted felon, you have to choose career paths where your background won't matter. Here is a sample list of careers for individuals that have a felony record.

- Construction equipment operator—salary $50,783 yearly
- Indusrial machine mechanic—$ 41,050 yearly
- Barbering and cosmetology—salary ranges between $15 and $19 per hour.
- Culinary arts—$16-$20 per hour.

- Automotive repair—$16-$26 per hour.
- Diesel mechanic—$14.90-$ 20.07 hour.
- Plumbing—$16.63-$26.27per hour.
- Welding—$17-$23per hour.
- Commercial electrician—$13-$38 per hour.

All the above-mentioned programs are excellent for ex-offenders. These are skills you can learn in a relatively short period of time, usually six months to a year, and the pay scale for these jobs are well above average.

If you are worrying about how to pay for your education, *don't*. The federal government will take care of that! As an American citizen, felony or not Uncle Sam will provide you with the necessary funds for you to go to school.

There are two types of grant programs available:

- Need-based grants
- Merit-based grants

If you are an ex-offender wanting to attend school, you are eligible for all need-based grants, which are the Federal Pell Grant and Federal Supplemental Education Opportunity Grant (FSEOG). The amount you may receive each year may change depending on the federal budget restrictions, family contributions, and your student status. Usually, most ex-felons don't have a lot of financial support from family after being released. In this case, you should receive the maximum distribution.

The Pell Grant was designed for all disadvantaged citizens who plan on attaining a secondary education.

The Federal Supplemental Education Opportunity Grant (FSEOG) is awarded to students with the most need. This grant is for students that have an expected family contribution of $0.

The Federal Work-Study Program is to help disadvantaged students *earn* money toward their college expenses. (This is a job where the federal government puts up the money to pay your wages while you work at the school.)

Get It! The Government Is Paying You to Work

Montgomery GI Bill is mainly for those who have served in any branch of the military.

Most states grant programs to individuals who wish to attend school. In GA, it's the HOPE Scholarship. Check with your local community college or technical school to see what other programs may be available in your state.

Applying for any grant program starts with the FAFSA application. You can apply online at FAFSA.com. The application is simple, and you can complete the process in less than thirty minutes.

If you haven't finished high school or received your GED certificate, some community colleges/technical schools will help with your GED once you enroll in one of their programs. For those who are still incarcerated, I suggest attaining your GED while in prison.

This will benefit you in more ways than one:

(A) It will help make the transition from prison to society much easier. It is a known fact that receiving an education helps with a person's coping abilities.
(B) By attaining your GED and applying for your federal grants in prison, you make going forward an easier process. You can literally move from a prison, into the classroom, right into the workplace, and earn money while doing it.

Note: As an ex-offender, another great way to overcome the odds is by learning another language. With the invention of the computer and Internet, most businesses have gone global. They operate in many different countries and employ individuals from diverse cultures. You can enhance your chances of getting hired if you are bilingual. Companies consider individuals who are bilingual to be a great asset to have on the team. In addition, having this ability will increase your chances for promotion in the future.

How to Get a Job with a Felony Record

There have been many blogs and books written by so-called experts concerning ex-felons. However, most of these individuals have never experienced what you are going through and can't truly relate to your difficulty.

The information, though well intentioned, lacks the answer to the universal question all ex-offenders are asking, "How do I get a job?" That is the only concern for those who have been recently released from prison and those who have past felony convictions on their record.

I have read many articles and books that stress having your record expunged before applying for a job. This is not bad advice, but it's not the right advice for most ex-offenders. Let me explain to you the various processes for clearing your record and which one's best for most individuals.

Expungement is simply the process of having erroneous information permanently removed from your record. Basically, you are petitioning the courts to have a criminal conviction removed from their record. This process is usually only granted to first-time offenders and have other restrictions such as the following:

- There is usually a five-year waiting period between the incident and expungement (waiting period may vary from state to state).
- Have no other incidents during the waiting period.
- All terms of sentence must be completed (no probation/parole).
- No pending cases.

There are some convictions that will exclude you from the expungement process: rape, sexual battery, delinquency of a minor, murder, and child molestation/pornography.

Check with your local clerk of courts for more details on this process.

A certificate of rehabilitation is a court order that states a convicted felon has been rehabilitated. (In my opinion, this is not worth the paper it's printed on.) Most employers don't consider this certificate as a valid representation of the ex-offender's character.

Any of the above is a good place to start for any ex-offender; however, I strongly recommend the process of having your record sealed.

What is record sealing? It is the process of having your record hidden from public view. In some states, those records are destroyed altogether. Once your record has been sealed, you can legally and honestly answer no when asked if you have ever been convicted of a felony. No one will have the ability to view your past convictions except the courts. Not your employer or the public. When a background check is performed, it will say, "No record found." I recommend this process because it provides the best results. The cost to have your record sealed varies from state to state but is generally $75-$125. This process is simple and can be done without the assistance of an attorney.

Building Your Own Brand

What is a brand? A brand is the identity of a specific product, service, or business. For you, it is your personality. It's who you are at the core.

Sounds crazy, but it is not! Consider this, companies like Coca-Cola, Pepsi, Nike, and Apple are very successful brands.

When you think of buying a soft drink, there are two brands that mainly come to mind: Pepsi or Coke. And if you don't buy any of the two, it's very likely that you will purchase another kind of soft drink that is under their corporate umbrella. Why? Because companies like these spend a lot of time and money in an effort to build their brand image, and just like those companies, you should also spend time and a little money building your brand.

As with a company, to be a successful brand, you must be genuine and authentic. In other words, you have to show yourself and the world around you that you are the real McCoy. Everything you do or don't do shows your core values. From the way you dress to how you carry yourself at home or in public, all these things represent your brand.

What is your brand? "You are!" Just like a company has a CEO, so it is with your life. You are essentially the CEO of your life. How it performs or doesn't perform is entirely up to you. Your life can be profitable or unprofitable, but at the end of the day, you are ultimately responsible for the decisions as to which direction your company is headed.

When you brand yourself, you are telling the world that when dealing with you, they are going to get something of quality. To your perspective employer, you are saying, "When you hire me, you will get the best return on your investment. I will deliver my work on time day in day out."

Building your own brand is important because word of mouth is the most effective form of advertising. What your friends, family, and the people you meet think and say about you means a lot. This is all a part of effective networking, and effective networking builds "influencing power."

Take a look at some of the fashionable clothing and perfume lines out there today. You have Jay-Z's Rocawear, P. Diddy's Sean John, Jennifer Lopez's JLO, and Ralph Lauren's Polo cologne. These are all examples of a brand's influencing power. They project a certain power and presence. That's why we go buy brands like this because we want to be associated with the brand's powerful presence. It's called the halo effect. It's the belief that when you wear that particular brand, some of that power will rub off on you. You begin to feel more confident about yourself, and this confidence transfers into other areas of your life.

If you want people to see you as a powerful brand, then you must act like a powerful leader. This means leading by example. If those around you can't see you running your brand (self) like a credible leader, then they are not going to want to be associated with you in any form.

On the streets as well as in prisons across the country, you hear the word *loyalty* spoken many times over, but do you know what real loyalty means? It means being *true* and *honest* to *yourself*. It means constantly trying to improve yourself through learning, growing, building right relationships, and delivering great results.

How do I build my brand? I had the opportunity to read an article that list ways you can build your own brand. Here are some things you can do to become a better you: Do a market analysis on yourself. Companies do analyses all the time to see where they are and to help project where they're headed. A good analysis can help you better understand your strong and weak points. It will tell you where you are right now and what you need to do to move forward. Before you continue reading, take a moment to do a market analysis on yourself. You will be amazed at what you can learn. Also, by working on this now, you will be better prepared during an interview.

The Market Analysis

Take a pen and a piece of paper. Form four columns! What you are going to do is make a list of your strengths, weaknesses, opportunities, and threats. Be honest with yourself during this process. If you are not honest with yourself, how can you be honest with others? This exercise will help you to make better decisions about what steps you should take to fine-tune your company (your life).

Once you have completed your list, use it to find ways for improving yourself. Ask yourself, What can I do to make me stand out more than the next person? If you can't answer this question in a way that grabs you, then you have a problem. If you can't give yourself a convincing answer, then how well do you think you will come across to an interviewer?

What qualities do you have that make you distinctive from the other job seekers?

What makes you so special?

How can you help the company perform better? It is important to be able to state how, if hired, your presence within that organization can help that company's bottom line. To be able to answer this question well during an interview could mean the difference in getting hired or not.

Most interviewers want to know, if they take the risk and hire you, what can you bring to the table that will benefit their organization? To be able to answer all these questions and a few more is essential in landing a job. That is why research is so important; it can make or break any business endeavor. It is also a good idea to revisit your market analysis on a regular basis to track your progress. This will help to make sure you stay on course.

Getting Ready for the Job You Want

When looking for a job, having a résumé is a must. A résumé is important for many reasons; the most important is the ease in which the interviewer can get a better understanding of your qualifications for the opening within the organization.

Your résumé should highlight your qualifications, work experience, and any education that you have that best suits the job you're applying for. A great suggestion is to explain your accomplishments for every position you've held in the past. Make sure you have well-prepared references. Many job seekers lose great opportunities for great jobs because of a lack of good references. When listing references, use credible individuals within the community, not your cousin Ron-Ron that works at the corner store. Use individuals like your pastor, former employer, or business owner. If you don't know anyone in these positions, use the best individuals you have available. References like these go a long way in helping you achieve a job. Good references show the interviewer that you are a person of quality despite your past mistakes and that you have people on your team that believe in you and are willing to vouch for your character.

Example: if you worked at ABC Corporation for the last four years, you should list your accomplishments at that organization along with information on how you helped your particular department cut costs or how you worked on the team that came up with a new idea that increased productivity.

Be truthful about your education and skills on your résumé because many companies will check to see if you have done what you said, and if you are caught in a lie, you will lose all credibility and an opportunity to work for that organization.

Another great idea is to learn all you can about a particular company and industry before the interview. Being well-informed will show the interviewer that you are serious about having an opportunity to work within the organization.

It's also important to make your résumé stand out from the rest, maybe include a nice border; this will help increase your chances of getting an interview.

Things to avoid in a résumé:

- Avoid major gaps in employment. If you do have a gap, then list why.
- If you have been incarcerated and worked during that time, list the jobs you performed during that period. Many prisons give inmates certificates of completion for work performed at the facility. Most certificates are from state community colleges and technical schools and will help in determining your ability to perform the job in which you are applying.
- No pictures of graphics. This can be distracting to the recruiter.
- Don't list any hobbies—just stick with your accomplishments.
- Use short paragraphs—long paragraphs can get your résumé tossed to the side.
- Limit your résumé to one page if possible, but no more than two.
- Make sure you date your employment history correctly—you want to make your résumé easy to read.
- Make sure your spelling and grammar are correct.

Now that you have done all the necessary steps needed to position yourself for success, it's time to begin your job search.

Set a Goal to Help You Reach the Top

A goal is something you are trying to do or achieve.

In life, it is important for individuals to set goals for themselves. A goal will help to keep you going when faced with difficult times. Without them, you can lose focus on what you are trying to accomplish. However, when setting your goal, make sure that it's realistic. Many people get discouraged when they don't accomplish their goals; often this is due to the goal being set beyond the individual's ability to achieve it. I'm not saying that anything is not possible, I'm only saying that your initial goals should reflect where you are in life and the resources you have at your disposal.

Here are four things you should do when setting your goals:

1. Set a goal that will stretch you but, at the same time, is realistic.
2. Make up your mind that you are going to accomplish it no matter what may get in your way.
3. Be flexible. If circumstances change, then don't be afraid to change directions in attaining your goal.
4. When you achieve it, reward yourself.

During your job search you may want to set goals such as "Today, I want to make ten phone calls to potential employers" or "I will go on five interviews this month."

Whatever your goal, it is a good idea is to write it down on paper then place it somewhere visible like on a mirror or refrigerator. By doing this, it will help you keep your eye on the prize. Also, make sure your goal is clear and that you have a plan in place to achieve it. Make sure your goal fits your lifestyle.

Example: If you have small children, you may need to set your goals with them in mind. If you live in a rural area where jobs are scarce, you may need to factor in how you are going to get to where you need to go to get the job.

Getting the Job You Want
When You Want It!

I was surfing the web one day and came across a great article on how to market yourself when looking for employment. I thought the article was very informative and decided to see if it would work, so I shared this unique approach with a few people. They went and applied the technique. To my astonishment, it worked better than I had expected. Two of the three individuals landed a job within a short period of time, and the other had a number of interviews scheduled. In fact, because of how well this technique worked, I decided to include it here for you.

We talked earlier about building your own brand. Well, a great way to help in that process is to advertise your skills using business cards. This may sound a little crazy, but it works. Let me give you an example of its effectiveness.

When looking for a job, just think about how many employment prospects you will come into contact with on a daily basis. For the sake of argument, let's say you come across seven prospects on any given day. Now let's say that you give your employment card to all seven prospects, which are thirty-five prospects in a five-day week. Those seven prospects tell two of their associates about your unorthodox approach for finding a job. That would mean in a week's time, your information will be in the hands of seventy employment prospects. Now let's assume you do this for a month. That would put your employment opportunities at 560 prospects per month. Now tell me, isn't this a great way of increasing your chances of finding a job in a relatively short period of time? This process allows you to cover a lot of ground without having to stretch yourself too thin.

These cards are inexpensive to have made, and any print shop can help with your request. The cost should be no more than $25-$30 but is well worth the investment. Your cards should list your skills and how those skills can help a business reach their goals. Most business cards have information on the front only, but I suggest using both front and back. This way, you can explain your skills and employment desires in more detail. You will be surprised at how well this form of marketing will help during your job campaign.

Business Card Sample

Doing this now will cause you to be better prepared when you are called for an interview.

James T. Smith	
Honest	
Dependable	
Hardworking	
Full or Part-time Position Desired	
5 years Commercial Carpentry Experience	
2 years Electrical Installation Experience	
(Phone) 404-555-5555	References Available
(Email) *jsmith@yahoo.com*	Bondable

Your card should give a short but accurate description of your skills and your willingness to showcase those skills to a potential employer. Use the back of the card to list any other skills you may possess and any computer knowledge you have, such as being proficient in Microsoft Word, Excel, etc.

Schedule Your Job Search

Much has been written about the best times to search for a job; however, through experience, I have found that the best day is every day. When I say "every day," I mean just that, every day. Any day, Monday through Sunday, that you are unemployed is a great day to be on the lookout for employment opportunities, especially on days when the weather is at its worst.

While the other job seekers are at home, you will be out taking advantage of their lack of initiative. Showing up on days like this says something positive about you. To your perspective employer it says you are dedicated, dependable, and don't mind working hard. A person like you doesn't allow adversity to get in the way of accomplishing what you set out to do.

When looking for a job, it is best to have a plan. There is a saying, "If you fail to plan, then you plan to fail." For you, failure is not an option. You have already been at the bottom for far too long, and now it's time to stay focused on what you are trying to achieve. What better way to make sure you stay on course than by making a schedule of the things you need to do in order to maximize your time and effort. I have provided for you a sample schedule that is designed to help with your job search. You can modify this schedule to fit your needs, but I highly suggest you stick to the plan I have here because its usefulness is universal and will work in every city across America.

Weekly Job Schedule

	6:30 AM	7:00 AM	8:00 AM	9:00 AM - 12:00 PM	12:00 PM - 1:00 PM	1:00 PM - 4:00 PM
MONDAY	GET UP/GET READY	BREAKFAST	START ORGANIZING YOUR MATERIAL	SEARCH THE CLASSIFIEDS/ START CALLING LEADS.	LUNCH	MAKE PHONE CALLS TO LEADS/GATHER INFORMATION ON JOB OPPORTUNITIES.
TUESDAY	GET UP/GET READY	BREAKFAST	START ORGANIZING YOUR MATERIAL	SEARCH THE CLASSIFIEDS/ START CALLING LEADS	LUNCH	NETWORKING
WEDNESDAY	GET UP/GET READY	BREAKFAST	START ORGANIZING YOUR MATERIAL	SEARCH THE CLASSIFIEDS/ START CALLING LEADS	LUNCH	NETWORKING
THURSDAY	GET UP/GET READY	BREAKFAST	START ORGANIZING YOUR MATERIAL	SEARCH THE CLASSIFIEDS/ START CALLING LEADS	LUNCH	NETWORKING
FRIDAY	GET UP/GET READY	BREAKFAST	START ORGANIZING YOUR MATERIAL	SEARCH THE CLASSIFIEDS/ START CALLING LEADS	LUNCH	NETWORKING
SATURDAY	GET UP/GET READY	BREAKFAST	START MAKING PHONE CALLS/ NETWORKING	GET OUT AND DEVELOP MORE LEADS THROUGH NETWORKING	NETWORKING	NETWORKING
SUNDAY	REST	REST	REST	REST	REST	REST

Notice that every day starts at 6:30 AM, followed by breakfast at 7:00 AM. The reason for this is simple. Getting up at 6:30 AM will give you the extra time you need to get ready and to organize your material for that day. Searching for a job takes energy. A proper breakfast will give you the fuel you need to function at your maximum potential. If there is one thing you want to avoid, it's waking up and not finding your car keys, not having clothes ready, not having enough time to get where you're going due to traffic conditions, and having your stomach on empty.

Also, if you start your day without giving your body the proper nutrients it needs to function, you are essentially starting with the wrong foundation, and this can cause your whole day to go off track.

When beginning your search, I recommend getting all your things together the night before. Doing this will cause you to have fewer problems the following morning.

I told you about using business cards to promote yourself during the initial start of your job hunt. Another useful tool is your local newspaper. Today, the majority of job seekers have come to rely heavily on the Internet, overlooking the everyday paper. This leaves you with a great opportunity because there are still many companies that use the local newspaper in the advertisement of job openings, especially small businesses.

A few other places that will help in your search are as follows:

Temporary day-labor agency. This is a good way of finding a job. Most don't take you through the hassles about your background. They are more concerned with your ability to do the job. I recommend agencies like *Labor Ready*, *Labor Finders*, and *Manpower*. Most assignments are temporary, day-to-day assignments, and you usually get paid daily. If you perform well on the job, the client may decide to keep you on long term, which could result in you getting hired.

State department of labor. This is another place to find employment. I suggest visiting your state labor department's website. Go to job search. Then search for jobs that fit your skills. Many ex-offenders have found jobs using this service by matching their skills to the right job. If you have extensive knowledge in a particular field, some employers will find a way to work around your record.

Social networking sites. Most people visit sites such as Facebook, MySpace, Twitter, and YouTube. These social networking sites are a great way to advertise yourself for a job, especially if you are willing to relocate. The process is simple. Just use your cell phone or digital camera to make a short video of yourself that highlights your skills and position desired. My nephew did this and has made over $20,000 to date.

One ex-felon I know had just been released from prison after serving ten years. He had been searching for a job since his release but found nothing. I ran into him at a local supermarket, where he told me about his situation. I told him to try looking for his next job using this technique I'm about to share with you.

Work part-time instead of full-time. I have spoken with a lot of human resource managers about why they don't hire ex-felons and was told by more than a few that it was due to insurance purposes. I was told that the insurance companies won't insure ex-felons due to their high-risk factor, which is basically saying they are nothing but trouble. When I heard this, a light went off in my brain. I thought to myself, *What if the ex-felon only worked part-time?* I asked a friend of mine who was a manager at a large manufacturing firm about the possibility of an ex-felon gaining employment within her firm as long as the employee didn't work full-time. She confirmed what I had been thinking. She said that as long as the person worked part-time, they would not have to worry about experiencing problems from the insurance companies, which would allow them greater leeway during the hiring process if they felt the person had changed and possessed the skills that the company needed.

Manufacturing plants. They are gold mines for ex-felons, especially processing companies. Many of these companies hired a multitude of illegal immigrants in the past to take advantage of cheap labor. However, in recent years, the federal as well as state governments have begun to crack down on illegals in our country, which in turn has created tremendous opportunities for ex-felons. These companies will need people to fill those positions fast in order to keep up productivity and are willing to give ex-offenders a chance. Most jobs start at above-average pay but offer excellent opportunities for advancement. I know one gentleman who was recently released from prison after serving twenty-three years for murder. He went and applied at a poultry plant in East Georgia, and within an hour after filling out the application, they were calling him in for an interview. He started the job the following Monday.

Small companies. They are good places for ex-felons to look for job opportunities because these companies are usually family owned and family operated. Situations like this will give you an excellent opportunity to sell yourself because the person giving the interview is usually the owner or at least have a say in who ultimately gets hired. This is the best-case scenario for highlighting your skills and making a lasting impression.

Moving companies. They are great sources for employment. The work is hard, the hours long, which is why most job seekers avoid them. These companies are a gold mine for an ex-offender! Most don't require a background check, and the ones that do are very lenient with individuals who have made past mistakes. (Red-hot advice: Get up! Get the phone book and start calling these companies now!)

Local union organizations. These organizations often have a list of companies that hire ex-offenders. Utilizing them would help increase your chances of finding a job.

Get Work Ready certified. Many employers are requiring potential employees to possess the necessary skill level to perform the job advertised. Tests such as these ensure that the state's workforce has the best skills and training for world-class job opportunities.

Earning your Work Ready certificate will verify your work readiness skill level to potential employers and demonstrates your commitment to success.

How this will help you:

- Shows you have the skills and work habits that meet the needs of employers.
- You stand above other job applicants that don't have it.
- Determines where you need improvement.
- Increases your opportunity for promotions.
- Submitting along with your résumé increases your chances of getting the job.

To earn your certificate, contact your state department of labor. The cost is *free*!

The Interview

We have covered quite a bit of information on how to get the job you want. You have already taken the steps toward landing an interview; now here comes the call you have been waiting for. Here are a few tips to help you overcome any obstacles that may arise during the interview stage.

Practice—there is no better way to prepare for an interview than to practice. Get a friend or family member to act as the interviewer. During this session, have them ask you questions that may arise during the interviewing process, such as "I see you have a felony on your record. May I ask what happened? How have you changed since the incident?" Expect these questions, and make sure you have an appropriate answer. For a question like this, you want to address it in a way that shows you have learned from your past mistakes and have put that lifestyle behind you. After that, highlight the positive things you have done since the incident to improve your life. What you want to do during the interview is distance yourself as far as possible from the old you while highlighting the skills of the new you.

Dress appropriately for the job you are applying for. Don't wear sagging pants or shirts that hang too loosely. To be safe, wear a pair of khakis with a nice shirt tucked into your pants. Remember, most people go by first impressions, so make yours the best possible.

On the day of the interview, make sure you give yourself enough time to get to where you have to go. Arriving fifteen minutes early is a plus when going to an interview. This shows your punctuality and eagerness to get the job. Showing up late for an interview can be the difference between getting the job or not.

When greeting the interviewer, give a firm handshake. This shows confidence. Don't be overly aggressive when shaking hands; it could be viewed the wrong way.

During the interview, sit straight. Look the interviewer in the eyes when answering questions. Looking around the room when being asked a question could come off as if you are hiding something or, worse yet, not being truthful.

Answer the interviewer's questions clearly and honestly.

Creating Your Future

We have covered a lot of information on how to find a job; however, the best and most reliable way to obtain a job is to create one for yourself. With the economy in the state that it is in, many companies may hire today but lay off tomorrow, leaving you with a high level of uncertainty about your future. Not knowing whether you are going to have a job in the future can be quite nerve-racking; however, there is way to insulate yourself from this roller-coaster ride.

Start Your Own Business

Going into business for yourself is a tried-and-true method to avoid being scrutinized because of your past mistakes. It evens the playing field for the ex-offender and allows you the opportunity to be judged by your abilities and not your past. It also allows you total access to the consumer and labor markets without the hassle of being denied access to opportunities because of your background. When going into business for yourself, you take control of your destiny.

Throughout this book, I have stressed the importance of getting an education, and now I am doing it again. Why? Because knowledge is a foundational key to *success*. Obtaining knowledge about a particular subject increases your chances of finding a job; it's also a must when going into business for yourself. Earlier I mentioned a few fields of study that are excellent opportunities for ex-offenders. Now I'm going to teach you how to take what you know and move to the next level.

Planning for Your Future

Have you ever wondered why some people achieve their goals and why others fall short despite their efforts? The difference between the two is not a lack of talent, education, or motivation. The only difference there is between those who accomplish their goals and those who don't is simply a matter of *planning. Proper planning and executing what was planned is the key to making every endeavor a success.* For you to truly live a successful and rewarding life, you must properly plan your steps daily. Here are four areas of life that you must focus on in order for you to succeed in life: *dreams, values, goals,* and *strategies.*

In his book *Financial Defense,* Charles J. Givens said, "Your dreams are the destinations you want to reach; your goals are the signposts of accomplishment that define your life path. Your values set the limits for the time and energy you will choose to expend on any dream or goal, and your strategies are the tools of accomplishment. Together they become the blueprint for a rich, rewarding life." In order for you to have true satisfaction/success in anything you must first possess good *values.* What you value most in life will be reflected in your goals or accomplishments.

What are "values?" Simply put, your values are the things that really matter to you. They are the ideas and beliefs you believe are special so much so that they manifest themselves in your everyday life. Example: if you value the overall well-being of yourself and family, you will do whatever (legally) it takes to insure your overall well-being.

Values and the choices you make in life go hand in hand. If you say you value something (like a job) but your choices don't reflect what you say you value (not showing up for work on time), then the only outcomes will be continued frustration and dissatisfaction with life. When you act in accordance with your values, you will experience a sense of satisfaction and fulfillment. Making choices that are not in alignment with your values will bring about feelings of fear, frustration, and imbalance.

Exercise: take time now to identify what you value most in life. Tell you what! Instead of just thinking about it, I want you to write on paper the things that you value most.

Write down the seven things you value most, with the most important being number one. Keep on with your list until you reach number seven. Once completed, take ten minutes to review your list. Ask yourself this question, Do my choices really reflect the things I value most? If you answered yes, then congratulations, you're on the right track to a successful life. However, if you answered no and your choices don't reflect what you value most, then you need to make some adjustments.

"Eric, I don't know what my values are." Don't worry; there are many people just like you. It's not that you don't know what your values are but that you are having trouble identifying those values. If you don't know what you value most, here is a short list of important values that may help in building your own.

- Financial security
- Good health
- A better relationship with your mate/children
- Spiritual fulfillment
- Starting your own business
- Travel

Now that you have your list and have reviewed your values, ask yourself, Are there any areas on my list that may be destructive? Destructive values include wanting something for nothing in return, your wants and pleasure at the expense of those around you, and the desire to control others. All these are symptoms of destructive habits. Eliminating destructive values is essential in achieving the success you want in life. If not weeded out, they will drain energy from every area of your life; however, there is no quick exercise to getting rid of those habits. The only way to overcome them is by working on them constantly.

I asked you to write down your values list then asked if there were any you could identify as being destructive. Now I'm asking you to make a list of those destructive habits that are keeping you from living the life you deserve. Why am I asking you to do this? Because by making your list, you can now begin working on the symptoms that help to create those destructive values. Symptoms include alcohol, drugs, prejudice, blaming everyone for everything that goes wrong in your life, etc.

Once that's done, make a plan to get rid of those symptoms. Your plan should have a start and completion date. Get it in writing. Writing helps to bring what you are trying to accomplish into focus. If you can see it in your mind, you can do it in life. Be committed. Your plan is only as good as you make it. Nothing is perfect, not even your plan. There will be roadblocks to where you are trying to go. Your level of commitment will determine your ability to handle those roadblocks when they arise. You must say to yourself and to the world around you,

"I will never quit and will always go hard!"

Now that we know that having *right values* is the first step in developing a successful life, it's now time to move to the next step.

Goals are the accomplishments you strive for based on your inner values. Some goals can be accomplished in a relatively short period of time, like committing to submit five applications a day; and some can take a lifetime, such as retiring a millionaire by age fifty. One thing for certain is that your goals and values must be in alignment with one another for true success to be attained. When making your goal, it must first possess certain characteristics to be attainable:

1. *It must be in writing.* Writing on paper what you want makes it stick in your brain. It also allows you the opportunity to plan, organize, and take the necessary steps to achievement.
2. *Be specific.* When you define goals specifically like "I want to become a certified welder within two years" then begin the necessary steps to accomplish that goal, it will begin to manifest itself into your life.
3. *Have a start and completion date.* For your goal to be accomplished, you must have a start date and a time period when you intend to have it completed. This will act as a guide in showing where you are during your path to achievement.

As you are working toward your goals, remember that to achieve success, you must keep your mind focused on what you want and not on what you don't want. Focusing on life's negatives will lead to either delaying your goal or losing sight of it altogether. By having a clear mental picture of what you want and never letting go of that picture, you will always find a way to accomplish your desires.

Dreams are what you would do if your life had no limits. Having the right type of dreams can increase your chances of gaining what you what in the time frame you want it in by a thousandfold. This means that once you have determined what you want, it would now be important to begin to see yourself already having what it is you are trying to accomplish. In other words, believing you already possess what you want. Science has determined 80 percent of your ability to attract the life you want comes from having a clear mental picture of it in your mind. So take out another piece of paper and make a list of seven dreams you wish to accomplish. Having difficulty? Then ask yourself, what things would you do if money were no object? Again, writing on paper what you want will make it real to you. Once you've completed your list, check to see if your dream list reflects values and sense of self-worth. As you continue toward your goal, revert to your dream/values list from time to time to see if they're still the same. Sometimes, as we journey through life, our wants and desires change as we grow in knowledge and understanding.

Strategy is a plan of action. It is the direction you choose to take over a period of time in order to achieve your objective. To you strategy is about

- where you are trying to get to in the long run,
- what type of people you should spend your time with and what activities you should commit yourself to,
- what resources you will need to achieve your goals.

Having a strategy keeps your plan moving in the right direction. It allows you the ability to adjust to unforeseen circumstances that may arise. When planning your strategy, specify what actions you will take and when you will take them. Understand that a life without a strategy is like a ship without a rudder. It will still get you somewhere, but is that somewhere a place you really want to go? Also, nothing in life is written in stone. As you continue down life's path, you will have to continually redefine your strategy; however, a properly executed plan will bring your dreams into your horizon.

How I Did It

When I decided to go into business for myself, I did a lot of research concerning the ins and outs of what I wanted to do. I estimated the costs, which were minimal, then had my business cards and flyers made up. I was ready to get started. Off I went, passing out my business cards and canvassing the surrounding neighborhood with flyers. I just knew my phone would be ringing off the hook. There was nothing that could stop me now, I thought to myself.

A week went by and not one call from my business cards or flyers. I had quit my job, and money was running low. Now I began to panic! Had I made a mistake in venturing off to do my own thing? I thought to myself.

Another week of passing out flyers and still nothing. Now I was past the scared phase and had moved directly to *distressed*. At the start of what would have been my third week, I decided to abandon my game plan in exchange of contracting my services to another company.

Again I looked through my local newspaper and found a position that I believed fit my needs. I called to find out what I had to do to get started and was told by the secretary to go fill out an application and to be sure to bring my business license.

The next day, with business license and résumé in hand, I went to apply! After I had finished the application, I was told to have a seat because the manager would like to see me. After a few minutes, I was buzzed back to his office. As I walked, I had the confidence of a lion.

During our conversation, he told me everything I needed to hear. The only thing I needed to do now was to provide him with my proof of bonding, then I could start. I was on cloud nine!

As I left his office, there was a smile on my face. I was told that he would call me to schedule a training class. I waited and waited! Two days went by and no call. I decided to call to see what was going on and was told on more than one occasion that he wasn't in the office.

Finally, in desperation, I went to pay him a visit. I needed money and fast. When I arrived, I found out that the secretary wasn't lying when she said he hadn't been in; he had a series of training classes that week, but today was his last class, and he was returning to the office shortly. I decided to wait! When he walked in, he greeted me warmly, then motioned me to follow him into his office. He then pulled out a file that had my name on it and said, "Eric, I have some unfortunate news!" *Oh god*, I thought to myself. He opened the file, glanced over it a minute, then said, "We can't allow you to work with us due to a problem concerning your background check." I said to myself, "Not again!"

I would like to tell you that I just got up and left, but that would be a complete lie. The truth is, I began to beg like a child wanting candy in a candy store. As I begged, he just sat there quietly with no facial expression whatsoever. After saying everything I knew to say, explaining how I had paid my debt to society, put that old life behind me, and quit my job to strike out on my own because I wanted more out of life, I told him everything.

When I finally finished talking, twenty minutes had passed. And in that whole time, he didn't say a word. I finally saw that I was wasting my time; I jumped up and started toward the door. I kindly thanked him for his time as I stood in the doorway to leave. This is when he finally decided to speak. He said, "Come back in and close the door."

I was surprised but did what he had said. In that office, he told me that he sympathized with what I had been through and commended me on trying to do something more with my life. Then he told me that I was going about what I was trying to accomplish all wrong. He said that the way I was doing things would lead me to a dead end over and over again. That's when he took the time to tell me this.

"If you're having trouble finding a job or going into business for yourself due to something contained in your background, you should always take these steps to avoid the problem."

- *Get certified in your particular field*

You may possess skills in a particular area; however, you will need more if you are going to have any chance of making it today. Being certified by your state or professional association tells your prospective employer as well as the consumer that you adhere to the highest standards in your field. It says you possess the necessary skills to get the job done.

- *If you are going into business for yourself, get your business license*

As an individual going into business for yourself, it is important for you to obtain a DBA (doing business as) license. A DBA is the legal name other than your name that you are using to run your business. You can apply for your DBA at the county clerk's office where your business will be located. (Registration for a DBA requires a small fee.)

The benefits of a DBA:

- Legally operate and advertise under your business name.
- No other business within your state can use your name.
- Open bank accounts under you business name.
- Accept checks.
- Gives your business a professional look.

- *Get your business incorporated*

A corporation is a legal entity (separate from its owner or owners) that is established to do business, having its own privileges and liabilities that are separate from its owners. By law, a corporation is looked upon as if it were a person, having the same rights as a person.

Step 3 is the most important step in securing your future. By getting yourself incorporated, you become a legal entity. For example, Chris Andrews Inc. When you become a corporation, you get a corporate social security number called an EIN. This will help you when applying for employment (contracting), credit cards, apartments, home loans, business loans, etc.

Benefits of an EIN number:

- For individuals, it allows you to establish credit under your business name. This means you can get credit in your business name (even if you have bad personal credit).
- If you want to contract your services (skills), it shields you from having to use your social security number.
- It allows you to apply for a D-U-N-S number, which is required to register for government grants.

- An S corporation can only be taxed once, which allows you to pay yourself tax-free.

    (S corporations must file an income tax return; however, as a sole owner, you can be paid a salary without being subject to double taxation. Contact an attorney for more information on S corporations.)

The information I received in that day changed my life forever! I applied all the above into my business, and within no time, I was doing business with Fortune 500 companies, all without worrying about a background check. I received credit cards in my business name, which allowed me to build my business financially. Again I'm not speaking theoretically; I am speaking about personal experience.

Certified Green

According to the Obama administration, green jobs will grow by 52 percent over the next five years while other jobs will grow at about 15 percent. Another report done by the Michigan Department of Energy says that green jobs earn above-average wages.

Consumers and businesses across the country are becoming increasingly concerned about their carbon impact. This opens the door for you to enter into the niche market being green.

If you are going into business for yourself, it is important that you become knowledgeable of your industry's environmental impact. Doing this will not only help you avoid harming the environment but will also increase your customer base due to more consumers becoming aware of their carbon footprint as well as the businesses they choose to do business with. Here is a list of organizations that can help you to become certified green.

- www.lohas.com
- www.greenseal.org
- www.fsc.org

If you decide to continue to work for someone else, inquire about taking a "Green certified." This will help you with job security as well as when applying for future employment opportunities.

Government Grants

I have heard so many different things concerning grants for ex-offenders. There is this popular farce going around that says that because you have been incarcerated, you are entitled to money from Social Security due to you being considered disabled. Again a bunch of crap! The government is not giving anyone any money just because they have been to prison, no matter if it was once or you're considered a repeat offender. If this were true, Social Security would be bankrupt. There have also been rumors floating around that you can get money every month up to $1,500 because you have been incarcerated. Again not true!

Here I'm going to attempt to set the record straight as to what you can and cannot get from the government as an ex-offender.

Food stamps. They are provided by the federal government to all disadvantaged citizens. Disadvantaged means not having proper means to provide for yourself. As an ex-offender, you automatically qualify for this benefit under section 212(d)(5) of the INA. To apply is simple! In Georgia, visit *www.compass.ga.gov*. For all other states, contact your state division of family and children services. Some states may require you to participate in an employment or training program. Also, if you attend college or trade school, you may still be eligible.

Health-care benefits. As an ex-offender with a medical condition, you can qualify for medical benefits through the Social Security Administration.

Housing and Urban Development (HUD). This provides grants for convicted felons. These loans are designed to help an ex-offender purchase a home. Be mindful that these homes will have a mortgage that must be repaid, so make sure you have adequate income to make the payments. Contact HUD at *www.hud.gov*.

The Small Business Administration (SBA). This provides grants and loans to for the disadvantaged. You are required to a legal business, and as an owner you must possess management experience necessary to run the firm. The SBA also provides free mentoring workshops for business owners. Contact the SBA at *www.sba.gov*

In addition to federal money to help you start your own business, there are also many private organizations that will give you money to get you on your feet.

For those of you who are interested in helping other ex-offenders, I offer you the chance by using the material you have here to help educate others like us who are disadvantaged.

Get your credit on track. Having a good credit rating is essential in society today. Your credit rating is used to determine many aspects of your life such as the following:

- Shelter—when buying a home or renting an apartment, your credit is a determining factor on whether the bank or landlord will provide you with a place to live.
- Transportation—to buy a good car, you will need the best credit rating possible to ensure the lowest possible interest rate. The lower you interest rate, the lower your car payment, the less you have coming out of your pockets every month. In addition, there are many insurance companies that are using your credit rating when determining whether they will insure you or not.
- Employment—many employers conduct credit checks in addition to criminal background checks when determining qualified job applicants.
- Starting your own business—a large number of businesses require credit to help run efficiently and effectively. They use your credit rating in extending you their products or services. Also, when operating your business, you will need capital. Banks will use your credit to determine your financial strength as well as your ability to repay the loan.

How do I clean up bad credit?

1. Obtain a copy of your report from all three credit reporting agencies: TransUnion, Equifax, and Experian. I recommend Equifax.com. There is a small fee; however, some states will allow one free report per year. The reason all three reports are important is that one

report may contain information that isn't on another. This way, you have an opportunity to compare all three reports.

2. View your report to make sure there are no mistakes. Many times, individuals will find erroneous items on their reports that can be removed. Even if all information is correct, you still have a chance to get rid of the negative information. In this case, you will begin the process of disputing the negative information even if it is correct.

The process of disputing negative information requires a lot of writing. You will need to write a letter to each reporting agency to dispute the claim against you. If within thirty days the business does not respond or can't prove the claim, the negative info will be deleted from your credit report.

If you are denied the first time, don't give up. This process may have to be repeated a few times in order to achieve the desired results. If the claimant (business) responds the first time, they might not continue to respond every time they receive a request concerning your report. Taking the time to continually respond to your one particular file costs the business time and money. Most times, the amount owed isn't worth the man-hours needed to confirm your debt.

If after repeated attempts you can't resolve the issue, you have the right to include a personal statement to explain why the negative information shouldn't be reported on your credit report. If you have some money to spare, there are many credit repair companies out there that can help. However, before choosing one, I suggest you do some research to make sure the company is reputable.

Coming Soon

The Ultimate Business for Ex-Offenders
If You Want to Make a Guaranteed $500-$2,500 per
Month from Home with Virtually Nothing out of
Pocket, This Business Is for You.
Requires No Licensing
No Special Training
Guaranteed Income

www.ingramcontent.com/pod-product-compliance
Lightning Source LLC
Chambersburg PA
CBHW021906170526
45157CB00005B/1988